CW00409590

Plant That Name!

Plant That Name!

Compiled by Susan Purveur

Illustrations by Elizabeth Harbour

MICHAEL JOSEPH
LONDON

MICHAEL JOSEPH LTD

Published by the Penguin Group
27 Wrights Lane, London W8 5TZ
Viking Penguin Inc., 375 Hudson Street, New York, New York 10014, USA
Penguin Books Australia Ltd, Ringwood, Victoria, Australia
Penguin Books Canada Ltd, 10 Alcorn Avenue, Toronto, Ontario, Canada M4V 3B2
Penguin Books (NZ) Ltd, 182–190 Wairau Road, Auckland 10, New Zealand

Penguin Books Ltd, Registered Offices: Harmondsworth, Middlesex, England

First published in Great Britain 1996

1 3 5 7 9 10 8 6 4 2

Text copyright © Susan Purveur 1996
Illustrations copyright © Elizabeth Harbour 1996

Typeset in Centaur
Printed in the Far East by Imago Publishing Services Ltd

A CIP catalogue record for this book is available from the British Library

ISBN 0 7181 3955 0

The moral right of the author has been asserted

*Dedicated to my mother and David Purveur
without whom the seed of an idea would not have germinated,
taken root and blossomed.*

ACKNOWLEDGEMENTS

Alan Purveur

Christopher Palmer   Angela Harding

Kevin Barrett   Derek Harding

Peter Davies   Martin Hogbin

Caroline Dawnay   John Langley

Jenny Dereham   Ken Williams

NOTES ON SOURCE BOOKS

All About House Plants by William Davidson (Optimum Books 1994)

Guide to Creative Gardening: consultant ed. Allen Paterson (Reader's Digest 1984)

The Herb Handbook by Pamela Westland (The Apple Press 1991)

The Plant Finder (94/95 edition) compiled by Chris Philip (Headmain 1994)

Pocket Encyclopaedia of Organic Gardening: contributing editor Geoff Hamilton (Dorling Kindersley 1991)

R.H.S. Gardeners' Encyclopedia of Plants & Flowers: editor in chief Christopher Brickell (Dorling Kindersley 1992)

INTRODUCTION

There are myriad books and magazines to assist people to 'Name that Plant' but anyone wishing to 'Plant that Name' would not know where to start . . . until now.

I wanted to celebrate meeting a long-lost member of my family by planting something special in my garden. I knew that there were named plants available on the market (in fact, one is actually named after my mother) but I had great difficulty in finding them as they were invariably catalogued under their botanical or Latin names.

In compiling this book, my aim was to simplify the process of finding a named plant for anyone wishing to celebrate or commemorate any one of the following occasions: birthdays, weddings, anniversaries of all sorts, Mothering Sunday or even a memorial to a loved one who has died. They could also be used as a memento of a visit or as a thank-you present.

The list of plants was correct when the copy was delivered to the printers, but it is inevitable that some will be discontinued and others will be added.

NOTES ON THE USE OF THIS GUIDE

The compilation is designed as a general guide to named plants, i.e. cultivated varieties and hybrids which, in horticultural literature, are usually presented within single quotation marks, thus: *Rhododendron* 'Abegail'. To simplify the presentation, the quotation marks are omitted in this book.

The three columns identify the female name, the common name and the Latin name, and where one female name has more than one corresponding plant, these are listed alphabetically within the common name column.

I have included only female names because during my research it became clear that it is relatively uncommon for plants to be named after the chaps. On the first drafting of this list, I did include what male named plants I could find but the proportion in comparison was so low that I felt it did not warrant a specific section.

Understandably, not all garden centres will stock every plant and, indeed, some of the plants are only available from specialist growers. Therefore, once a name and corresponding plant has been decided upon, one of two courses of action may be taken:

Either contact a garden centre or nursery and use their expert knowledge to track down the plants in question for you; or

Consult one of the many plant books (see list of Source Books on page 6

— and *The Plant Finder* is of particular value in this respect; however, the Latin name of the plant must be employed when using this book) or seed and nursery catalogues for details of nurseries which will stock the plant or be able to send it to you by mail order.

Some of the plants are available as seed, and these are marked with an * in the lists. However, the full list is as follows:

Available from Chiltern Seeds (Tel: 01229 581137)

Grace	Clarkia/Godetia
Guinevere	Delphinium
Rose	Forget-me-not

Available from Dobies Seeds (Tel: 01803 616281)

Cherie	Clarkia/Godetia
Christine	Dahlia
Dawn	Anchusa
Rosamund	Lobelia
Susie	Black-eyed Susan
Ursula	French marigold

Available from Marshalls Seeds (Tel: 01945 583407)

Becky	Coneflower
Lulu	French marigold

Available from Thompson & Morgan Seeds (Tel: 01473 689757)

Annabelle	Sweet pea
Janie	French marigold

Susan Purveur, who was born and educated in Middlesex, says that her interest in gardening stems from when, at the age of nine, she entered her local flower show and promptly won first prize in the geranium class – much to the amazement and irritation of the adult entrants. She later became an avid reader of all things horticultural and is currently studying for her Royal Horticultural Society certificate. She is married with one son and lives in Aylesford in Kent.

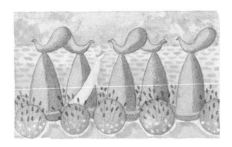

Elizabeth Harbour studied illustration at Maidstone College of Art and then at the Royal College of Art where, in 1991, she received the Princess of Wales Scholarship and also a National Magazine Award for Editorial Illustration. Her first book, produced while still studying at Maidstone, was the highly successful *A Gardener's Alphabet*, and her most recent work has been to provide the exceptional illustrations for *A First Picture Book of Nursery Rhymes*.

Abegail	Rhododendron (hybrid)	*Rhododendron*
Abigail	Violetta	*Viola*
Adele	Geranium	*Pelargonium*
Adelina	Viola	*Viola*
Adria	Fleabane	*Erigeron*
Agatha	Gallica rose	*Rosa*
Agnes	Hedgehog rose	*Rosa rugosa*
Agneta	Viola	*Viola*
Aida	Azalea	*Rhododendron*
Albertine	Rose (rambler)	*Rosa*
Alcea	Viola	*Viola*
Alethia	Violetta	*Viola*
Alex	Geranium	*Pelargonium*
Alexandra	Bougainvillea	*Bougainvillea*
Alexia	Viola	*Viola*
Alexis	Chrysanthemum	*Dendranthema*

Alice	Azalea	*Rhododendron*
	Cineraria	*Senecio bicolor cineraria*
	Double daisy	*Bellis perenni*
	Escallonia	*Escallonia*
	Gladioli	*Gladiolus*
	Pink	*Dianthus*
	Rhododendron (hybrid)	*Rhododendron*
Alison	Chrysanthemum	*Dendranthema*
	Geranium	*Pelargonium*
Allanah	Clematis	*Clematis* 'Jackmannii'
Alma	Geranium	*Pelargonium*
	Viola	*Viola*
Alys	Viola	*Viola*
Amanda	Cape primrose	*Streptocarpus*
	Houseleek	*Sempervivum*
	Rose (floribunda)	*Rosa*
Amber	Common holly	*Ilex*

Amelia	Geranium	*Pelargonium*
	Rose (damask)	*Rosa*
	Viola	*Viola*
Amethyst	False goat's beard	*Astilbe x arendsii*
Amy	Begonia	*Begonia*
	Hebe	*Hebe*
Anabell	Rose (floribunda)	*Rosa*
Anastasia	Chrysanthemum	*Dendranthema*
Andrea	Rose (miniature)	*Rosa*
Andromeda	Fuchsia	*Fuchsia*
Anette	Friendship plant	*Pilea involucrata*
Angela	Geranium	*Pelargonium*
Angelina	Rose (shrub)	*Rosa*
Angeline	Fuchsia	*Fuchsia*
Angelique	Fig	*Ficus carica*
	Geranium	*Pelargonium*
	Tulip	*Tulipa*
Anita	Rhododendron (hybrid)	*Rhododendron*
Anja	Phlox	*Phlox arendsii*
Ann	Lungwort	*Pulmonaria rubra*
	Magnolia	*Magnolia*
	Viola (exhibition)	*Viola*

Ann Marie	Hot-water plant	*Achimenes*
Anna	Clematis	*Clematis*
	Geranium	*Pelargonium*
	Heather	*Calluna vulgaris*
Anna Liza	Hyacinth	*Hyacinthus orientalis*
Anna Marie	Hyacinth	*Hyacinthus orientalis*
Annabel	Clematis	*Clematis*
	Fuchsia	*Fuchsia*
	Heather	*Calluna vulgaris*
	Rock rose	*Helianthemum*
Annabella	Azalea	*Rhododendron*
Annabelle	Geranium	*Pelargonium*
	Hydrangea	*Hydrangea arborescens*
	Pink	*Dianthus*
	Sweet pea*	*Lathyrus*
	Viola	*Viola*
Anne	Cape primrose	*Streptocarpus*
	Chrysanthemum	*Dendranthema*
	Primula	*Primula allionii*
Anne-Marie	Apple	*Malus domestica*

Anneke	Azalea	*Rhododendron*
	Heather	*Calluna vulgaris*
	Michaelmas daisy	*Aster novi-belgii*
	Tulip	*Tulipa*
Annemarie	Heather	*Calluna vulgaris*
Annette	Cinquefoil	*Potentilla fruticosa*
	Ivy	*Hedera helix*
Annie	Double daisy	*Bellis perennis*
Anny	Azalea	*Rhododendron*
Anthea	Daffodil	*Narcissus*
	Viola	*Viola*
	Yarrow	*Achillea*

Antoinette	Geranium	*Pelargonium*
Anuschka	Rhododendron (hybrid)	*Rhododendron*
Aphrodite	False goat's beard	*Astilbe simplicifolia*
	Geranium	*Pelargonium*
	Snake's head fritillary	*Fritillaria meleagris*
Arabella	Camellia	*Camellia japonica*
	Clematis	*Clematis*
	Viola	*Viola*
Ariane	Creeping phlox	*Phlox stolonifera*
Arianna	Clarkia/Godetia	*Clarkia (syn. Godetia)*
Astrid	Daphne	*Daphne burkwoodii*
	Viola	*Viola*
Audrey	Geranium	*Pelargonium*
	Michaelmas daisy	*Aster novi-belgii*
Augusta	Geranium	*Pelargonium*
Ayesha	Hydrangea	*Hydrangea macrophylla*

Babs	Chrysanthemum	*Dendranthema*
Barbara	Fuchsia	*Fuchsia*
	Viola	*Viola*
Bea	Hot-water plant	*Achimenes*
Beatrice	Alpine auricula	*Primula auricula*
	Hebe	*Hebe*
	Violetta	*Viola*
Beatrix	Geranium	*Pelargonium*
Becky	Coneflower*	*Rudbeckia*
Belinda	Amaryllis	*Hippeastrum*
Bella	Fuchsia	*Fuchsia*
Belle	Chrysanthemum	*Dendranthema*
Bernadette	Fuchsia	*Fuchsia*
	Heather	*Calluna vulgaris*
Bernice	Bellflower	*Campanula trachelium*
	Hot-water plant	*Achimenes*

Beryl	Cape primrose	*Streptocarpus*
	Daffodil	*Narcissus*
Bess	Geranium	*Pelargonium*
Beth	Pear	*Pyrus communis*
Bethany	Daffodil	*Narcissus*
	Houseleek	*Sempervivum*
Bettina	Polka dot plant	*Hypoestes phyllostachya*
	Rose (hybrid tea)	*Rosa*
	Saxifrage	*Saxifraga x paulinae*
	Viola	*Viola*
Betty	Azalea	*Rhododendron*
	Magnolia	*Magnolia*
	Phlox	*Phlox subulata*
	Viola	*Viola*
Beverley	Fuchsia	*Fuchsia*
Bianca	Fuchsia	*Fuchsia*
	Geranium	*Pelargonium*
	Prairie mallow	*Sidalcea*
	Violetta	*Viola*

Blanche	Rock rose	*Cistus*
Blossom	New Zealand tea tree	*Leptospermum scoparium*
Bobby	Pink	*Dianthus*
Bonny	Everlasting flower	*Acroclinium*
	Fuchsia	*Fuchsia*
	Iris	*Iris*
Brenda	Fuchsia	*Fuchsia*
	Geranium	*Pelargonium*
	Pyrethrum	*Tanacetum coccineum*
Bridget	Chrysanthemum	*Dendranthema*
	Saxifrage	*Saxifraga x edithiae*
Bridgette	Michaelmas daisy	*Aster novi-belgii*
Brigette	Ivy	*Hedera helix*
Brigitte	Rhododendron (hybrid)	*Rhododendron*
Brooke	Plantain lily	*Hosta*
Bunty	Alpine auricula	*Primula auricula*
	Chrysanthemum	*Dendranthema*

Cally	Geranium	*Pelargonium*
Camilla	Alpine auricula	*Primula auricula*
	Geranium	*Pelargonium*
	Pink	*Dianthus*
Camille	Dumb cane	*Dieffenbachia*
Candida	Dumb cane	*Dieffenbachia*
	Goat's rue	*Galega*
	Violetta	*Viola*
	Weigela	*Weigela*
Candy	Geranium	*Pelargonium*
	Hebe	*Hebe*
Carina	Violetta	*Viola*
Carlotta	Pink	*Dianthus*
Carmen	Auricula	*Primula x pubescens*
	Border carnation	*Dianthus*
Carmen	Heather	*Calluna vulgaris*

Carmen	Houseleek	*Sempervivum*
	Lily	*Lilium*
	Paeony	*Paeonia lactiflora*
	Rhododendron (hybrid)	*Rhododendron*
	Rose (rambler)	*Rosa*
Carmina	Polka-dot plant	*Hypoestes*
		phyllostachya
Carol	Cape primrose	*Streptocarpus*
	Paeony	*Paeonia*
	Plantain lily	*Hosta fortunei*
Carol Ann	Thyme	*Thymus x citriodorus*
Carole	Alpine auricula	*Primula auricula*
	Regal pelargonium	*Pelargonium*
Caroline	Clematis	*Clematis*
	Fuchsia	*Fuchsia*
	Viola	*Viola*
	Wisteria	*Wisteria sinensis*
Carolyn	Geranium	*Pelargonium*
	Heather	*Calluna vulgaris*
Carrie	Plantain lily	*Hosta sieboldii*
Cary Ann	Rhododendron (hybrid)	*Rhododendron*
Cassandra	Violetta	*Viola*

Catherina	Gooseberry	*Ribes uva-crispa*
Catherine	Apple	*Malus domestica*
	Auricula (double)	*Primula auricula*
	Heather	*Calluna vulgaris*
Cecile	Azalea	*Rhododendron*
	Fuchsia	*Fuchsia*
Cecilia	Bristle-cone pine	*Pinus aristata*
Cecily	Michaelmas daisy	*Aster novi-belgii*
Céleste	Rose	*Rosa*
Celia	Geranium	*Pelargonium*
Célina	Rose (moss)	*Rosa*
Chantal	Violetta	*Viola*
Charity	Fleabane	*Erigeron*
	Mahonia	*Mahonia lomariifolia*
Charlean	Camellia	*Camellia williamsii*
Charlene	Primrose (double)	*Primula*

Charmaine	Phlox	*Phlox paniculata*
	Rhododendron (hybrid)	*Rhododendron*
Charmian	Rose (shrub)	*Rosa*
Chastity	Pink	*Dianthus*
Chelsea	Black mulberry	*Morus nigra*
Cherie	Clarkia/Godetia*	*Clarkia* (syn. *Godetia*)
	Geranium	*Pelargonium*
Cherry	Geranium	*Pelargonium*
	Guzmania	*Guzmania*
	Primrose	*Primula*
Cheryl	Pink	*Dianthus*
Chloe	Auricula (show)	*Primula auricula*
	Violetta	*Viola*
Christabel	Gladioli	*Gladiolus*
	Hebe	*Hebe*
Christina	Arum lily	*Zantedeschia*
	Azalea	*Rhododendron*
	Heather	*Calluna vulgaris*
	Michaelmas daisy	*Aster novi-belgii*
Christine	Dahlia*	*Dahlia*
Christobel	Viola	*Viola*

Cindy	Geranium	*Pelargonium*
	Gladioli	*Gladiolus*
	Pink	*Dianthus*
	Viola	*Viola*
Clair	Geranium	*Pelargonium*
Clara	Begonia	*Begonia rex*
	Perpetual carnation	*Dianthus*
Clare	Daffodil (jonquil)	*Narcissus*
	Geranium	*Pelargonium*
	Houseleek	*Sempervivum*
	Oleander	*Nerium oleander*
	Orchid	*Pleione formosana*
	Pink	*Dianthus*
Clarinda	Border carnation	*Dianthus*
Clarissa	Geranium	*Pelargonium*
	Rose (miniature)	*Rosa*
Claudette	Geranium	*Pelargonium*
Claudia	Chrysanthemum	*Dendranthema*
Cleo	Iris	*Iris*
	Viola	*Viola*
Cleopatra	Begonia	*Begonia*

Clio	Rhododendron (hybrid)	*Rhododendron*
	Rose (perpetual)	*Rosa*
Clodagh	Viola	*Viola*
Clorinda	Geranium	*Pelargonium*
Columbine	Clematis	*Clematis alpina*
	Gladioli	*Gladiolus*
Connie	Fuchsia	*Fuchsia*
	Viola	*Viola*
Constance	Aster	*Aster ericoides*
	Clematis	*Clematis alpina*
	Fuchsia	*Fuchsia*
	Pink	*Dianthus*
Cora Ann	Daffodil (jonquil)	*Narcissus*

Coral	Auricula (show)	*Primula auricula*
Coralie	Rose (damask)	*Rosa*
	Violetta	*Viola*
Cordelia	Snowdrop (double)	*Galanthus*
	Viola	*Viola*
Corina	Lily	*Lilium*
Cornelia	Rose (hybrid musk)	*Rosa*
Cressida	Rose (shrub)	*Rosa*
Cynthia	Cape primrose	*Streptocarpus*
	Geranium	*Pelargonium*
	Lady tulip	*Tulipa clusiana*
	Rhododendron (hybrid)	*Rhododendron*

Dagmar	Rhododendron (hybrid)	*Rhododendron*
Daniela	Michaelmas daisy	*Aster novi-belgii*
Daphne	Chrysanthemum	*Dendranthema*
	Pink	*Dianthus*
	Rhododendron (hybrid)	*Rhododendron*
Darlene	Clematis	*Clematis*
Davina	Geranium	*Pelargonium*
	Viola	*Viola*
Dawn	Anchusa*	*Anchusa*
	Border carnation	*Dianthus*
	Clematis	*Clematis*
	Daffodil	*Narcissus*
	Fuchsia	*Fuchsia*
	Heather	*Erica versicolor*
	Plantain lily	*Hosta*
	Rhodohypoxis	*Rhodohypoxis*

Dawn *cont.*	Viburnum	*Viburnum x bodnantense*
	Violetta	*Viola*
Debbie	Camellia	*Camellia x williamsii*
	Hebe	*Hebe*
Debby	Fuchsia	*Fuchsia*
Deborah	Fuchsia	*Fuchsia*
	Norway maple	*Acer platanoides*
	Pittosporum	*Pittosporum tenuifolium*
Delia	Daffodil	*Narcissus*
	Viola	*Viola*
Delicia	Violetta	*Viola*
Delilah	Fuchsia	*Fuchsia*
	Geranium	*Pelargonium*
Della	Geranium	*Pelargonium*
Delphine	Viola	*Viola*
Denise	Chrysanthemum	*Dendranthema*
	Paeony	*Paeonia lactiflora*
Desdemona	Ligularia	*Ligularia dentata*
	Viola	*Viola*

Desmonda	Viola	*Viola*
Di	Geranium	*Pelargonium*
Diana	Freesia	*Freesia*
	Fuchsia	*Fuchsia*
	Hibiscus	*Hibiscus syriacus*
	Ivy	*Hedera helix*
	Michaelmas daisy	*Aster novi-belgii*
	Staff vine	*Celastrus orbiculatus*
	Tulip	*Tulipa*
	Viburnum	*Viburnum carlesii*
Diane	Alpine auricula	*Primula auricula*
	Geranium	*Pelargonium*
	Japanese larch	*Larix kaempferi*
	Pink	*Dianthus*
	Rhododendron (hybrid)	*Rhododendron*
	Witch Hazel	*Hamamelis x intermedia*

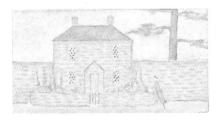

Dianne	Primula	*Primula x forsteri*
Dolly	Michaelmas daisy	*Aster novi-belgii*
Dominique	Arum lily	*Zantedeschia*
	Lily	*Lilium*
Donna	Chrysanthemum	*Dendranthema*
	Clematis	*Clematis*
Doreen	Paeony	*Paeonia lactiflora*
	Rose (hybrid tea)	*Rosa*
Doris	Pink	*Dianthus*
	Chrysanthemum	*Dendranthema*
Dorothea	Rhododendron (hybrid)	*Rhododendron*
Dorothy	Crocus (spring)	*Crocus chrysanthus*
	Fuchsia	*Fuchsia*
	Iris	*Iris laevigata*
	Plantain lily	*Hosta*
	Polyanthus	*Primula*
	Treasure flower	*Gazania*
Dot	Hot-water plant	*Achimenes*
Dulcie	Geranium	*Pelargonium*
	Rhodohypoxis	*Rhodohypoxis baurii*

Edith	Clematis	*Clematis*
	Cuckoo flower	*Cardamine pratensis*
	Fuchsia	*Fuchsia*
	Saxifrage	*Saxifraga x edithiae*
	St John's-wort	*Hypericum olympicum*
Edith Sarah	Gentian	*Gentiana sino-ornata*
Edna	Pink	*Dianthus*
Eileen	Pink	*Dianthus*
Eleanor	Gentian	*Gentiana*
	Geranium	*Pelargonium*
Eleanore	Rhododendron (hybrid)	*Rhododendron*
Elina	Rose (hybrid tea)	*Rosa*
Elinor	Lilac	*Syringa x prestoniae*
Elisabeth	Camellia	*Camellia japonica*

Elizabeth	Azalea	*Rhododendron*
	Bougainvillea	*Bougainvillea x*
		spectabilis
	Cinquefoil	*Potentilla*
		fruticosa
	Clematis	*Clematis* montana
	Fuchsia	*Fuchsia*
	Gentian	*Gentiana*
	Magnolia	*Magnolia*
	Michaelmas daisy	*Aster novi-belgii*
	Pink	*Dianthus*
	Rhododendron (hybrid)	*Rhododendron*
	Viola	*Viola*
Ellen	Chrysanthemum	*Dendranthema*
	Plantain lily	*Hosta*
	Rose (shrub)	*Rosa*
Elma	Rock rose	*Cistus*

Elsa	Fuchsia	*Fuchsia*
Elsbeth	Bloody cranesbill	*Geranium sanguineum*
Elsi	Cape primrose	*Streptocarpus*
Elsie	Alpine auricula	*Primula auricula*
	Geranium	*Pelargonium*
Elsie May	Alpine auricula	*Primula auricula*
Elspeth	Rhododendron (hybrid)	*Rhododendron*
Elvira	Daffodil	*Narcissus*
	Gladioli	*Gladiolus*
Emanuela	Rhododendron (hybrid)	*Rhododendron*
Emilie	Cinquefoil	*Potentilla*
Emily	Daffodil	*Narcissus*
	Rose (shrub)	*Rosa*
Emma	Geranium	*Pelargonium*
	Viola	*Viola*
Emma Lou	Chrysanthemum	*Dendranthema*
Emma Louise	Fuchsia	*Fuchsia*
Ena	Geranium	*Pelargonium*
Erica	False goat's beard	*Astilbe x arendsii*
	Michaelmas daisy	*Aster novi-belgii*
Erika	Hinoki cypress	*Chamaecyparis obtusa*
	Spiked speedwell	*Veronica spicata*
Estelle Marie	Fuchsia	*Fuchsia*
Ester	Ivy	*Hedera helix*

Esther	Aster	*Aster ericoides*
	Saxifrage	*Saxifraga x burnatii*
	Tulip	*Tulipa*
Ethel	Rhododendron (hybrid)	*Rhododendron*
Eugenie	Primrose (double)	*Primula*
	Windflower	*Anemone hupehensis*
Eurydice	Fuchsia	*Fuchsia*
Eva	Golden marguerite	*Anthemis cretica*
	Ivy	*Hedera helix*
	Michaelmas daisy	*Aster novi-belgii*
	Paeony	*Paeonia lactiflora*
	Phlox	*Phlox douglasii*
	Rose (hybrid musk)	*Rosa*
Evangeline	Rose (rambler)	*Rosa*
Eveline	Dahlia	*Dahlia*
	Hebe	*Hebe*
Evelyn	Penstemon	*Penstemon*
	Rose (shrub)	*Rosa*
Evita	Weigela	*Weigela*

Faith	Camellia	*Camellia japonica*
	Mahonia	*Mahonia lomariifolia*
	Michaelmas daisy	*Aster novi-belgii*
Fanny	Azalea	*Rhododendron*
Fatima	Camellia	*Camellia japonica*
Felicia	Rose (hybrid musk)	*Rosa*
Felicity	Fleabane	*Erigeron*
	Michaelmas daisy	*Aster novi-belgii*
	Viola	*Viola*
Fenella	Delphinium	*Delphinium*
Fergie	Fuchsia	*Fuchsia*
Fiona	Cape primrose	*Streptocarpus*
	Fuchsia	*Fuchsia*
	Pink	*Dianthus*
	Rose (shrub)	*Rosa*
	Viola	*Viola*

Flavia	Fuchsia	*Fuchsia*
Flora	Rose (rambler)	*Rosa*
Florence	Wild cherry	*Prunus avium*
	Viola	*Viola*
Frances	Bellflower	*Campanula persicifolia*
	Bell heather	*Erica cinerea*
	Eucodonia	*Eucodonia verticillata*
Francesca	Rose (hybrid musk)	*Rosa*
	Viola	*Viola*
Frankie	Clematis	*Clematis alpina*
Freda	Auricula (show)	*Primula auricula*
	Clematis	*Clematis montana*
	Pink	*Dianthus*
Freya	Geranium	*Pelargonium*

Gabrielle	Clematis	*Clematis*
Gail	Larch	*Larix leptolepis*
Garnet	Geranium	*Pelargonium*
Gemma	Geranium	*Pelargonium*
	Viola	*Viola*
Georgette	Gladioli	*Gladiolus*
Georgina	Viola	*Viola*
Geraldine	Geranium	*Pelargonium*
	Rose (floribunda)	*Rosa*
	Violetta	*Viola*
Gertrude	Chrysanthemum	*Dendranthema*
Gilda	Daffodil	*Narcissus*
	Fuchsia	*Fuchsia*
	Geranium	*Pelargonium*
	Rose (floribunda)	*Rosa*

Gill	Geranium	*Pelargonium*
Gillian	Gladioli	*Gladiolus*
	Hebe	*Parahebe x bidwillii*
Gina	Geranium	*Pelargonium*
	Violetta	*Viola*
Giselle	Viola	*Viola*
Gladys	Chrysanthemum	*Dendranthema*
	Rhododendron (hybrid)	*Rhododendron*
	Saxifrage	*Saxifraga*
Gloria	Cape primrose	*Streptocarpus*
	Chrysanthemum	*Dendranthema*
	False goat's beard	*Astilbe arendsii*

Gloria	Geranium	*Pelargonium*
	Saxifrage	*Saxifraga burseriana*
Goldie	Geranium	*Pelargonium*
	Oriental poppy	*Papaver orientale*
Grace	Clarkia/Godetia*	*Clarkia (syn. Godetia)*
	Viola	*Viola*
Gracie	Alpine auricula	*Primula auricula*
Greta	Auricula (show)	*Primula auricula*
	Azalea	*Rhododendron*
Guinevere	Delphinium*	*Delphinium elatum*
Gwen	Heather	*Erica versicolor*
Gwenda	Azalea	*Rhododendron*

Hanna	Fuchsia	*Fuchsia*
Hazel	Alpine auricula	*Primula auricula*
	Chrysanthemum	*Dendranthema*
	Fuchsia	*Fuchsia*
	Geranium	*Pelargonium*
	Ivy	*Hedera helix*
	Plantain lily	*Hosta*
	Treasure flower	*Gazania*
Heather	Michaelmas daisy	*Aster novi-belgii*
Heidi	Cape primrose	*Streptocarpus*
	Columnea	*Columnea*
	Geranium	*Pelargonium*
	Pink	*Dianthus*
Helen	Auricula (show)	*Primula auricula*
	Cape primrose	*Streptocarpus*
	Michaelmas daisy	*Aster novi-belgii*

Helen	Pink	*Dianthus*
	Viola	*Viola*
Helena	Auricula (show)	*Primula auricula*
	Geranium	*Pelargonium*
	Irish ivy	*Hedera hibernica*
	Viola	*Viola*
Helene	Gladioli	*Gladiolus*
	Hibiscus	*Hibiscus rosa-sinensis*
Helga	Austrian pine	*Pinus nigra nigra*
	Dahlia	*Dahlia*
Helge	Iris	*Iris*
Henriette	Dahlia	*Dahlia*
Hermione	Geranium	*Pelargonium*
	Nemesia	*Nemesia*
Hester	Heather	*Calluna vulgaris*
	Houseleek	*Sempervivum*

Hetty	Bellflower	*Campanula persicifolia*
	Heather	*Calluna vulgaris*
Hilda	Phlox	*Phlox x arendsii*
	Wood anemone	*Anemone nemorosa*
Hildegarde	Iris (Dutch)	*Iris*
Hippolyta	Snowdrop	*Galanthus*
Hippolyte	Gallica rose	*Rosa*
Holly	Chrysanthemum	*Dendranthema*
Hope	Camellia	*Camellia x williamsii*
Hyacinth	False goat's beard	*Astilbe x arendsii*
	Penstemon	*Penstemon*

Ida	Fuchsia	*Fuchsia*
	Iris	*Iris reticulata*
Ina	Pink	*Dianthus*
India	Hot-water plant	*Achimenes*
Inga	Wild cherry	*Prunus avium*
Ingrid	Ivy	*Hedera helix*
Iolanthe	Magnolia	*Magnolia*
Irene	Chrysanthemum	*Dendranthema*
	Geranium	*Pelargonium*
	Michaelmas daisy	*Aster novi-belgi*
Iris	Dahlia (pompon)	*Dahlia*
	Orchid	*Pleione formosana*
Isabel	Bellflower	*Campanula carpatica*

Isabelina	Foxglove	*Digitalis purpurea*
Isabella	Lilac	*Syringa x prestoniae*
Isobel	Rose (hybrid tea)	*Rosa*
Ivette	Azalea	*Rhododendron*

Jackie	Mullein	*Verbascum*
Jacqueline	Geranium	*Pelargonium*
	Schefflera	*Schefflera arboricola*
	Tulip	*Tulipa*
Jacquetta	Rhododendron (hybrid)	*Rhododendron*
Jade	Rhododendron (hybrid)	*Rhododendron*
Jan	Heather	*Calluna vulgaris*
Jane	Houseleek	*Sempervivum*
	Magnolia	*Magnolia*
Janet	Bell heather	*Erica cinerea*
	Plantain lily	*Hosta fortunei*
	Primula	*Primula marginata*
	Viola	*Viola*
Janie	French marigold*	*Tagetes patula*
Janine	Violetta	*Viola*
Janna	Viola	*Viola*

Jasmine	Regal Pelargonium	*Pelargonium*
Jay	Geranium	*Pelargonium*
Jayne	Geranium	*Pelargonium*
Jean	Fuchsia	*Fuchsia*
	Michaelmas daisy	*Aster novi-belgii*
	Rhododendron (hybrid)	*Rhododendron*
Jeanette	Azalea	*Rhododendron*
	Dumb cane	*Dieffenbachia*
Jeannie	Penstemon	*Penstemon*
	Viola	*Viola*
Jeannine	Allium	*Allium moly*
	Crocus	*Crocus chrysanthus*
	Erythronium	*Erythronium*
	Iris (Reticulata)	*Iris*
Jelena	Witch hazel	*Hamamelis x intermedia*
Jemma	Viola	*Viola*
Jennifer	Geranium	*Pelargonium*
	Kaffir lily	*Schizostylis coccinea*
Jenny	Alpine auricula	*Primula auricula*
	Daffodil	*Narcissus*

Jenny	Heather	*Calluna vulgaris*
	Kiwi fruit	*Actinidia deliciosa*
	Michaelmas daisy	*Aster novi-belgii*
	Rhododendron (hybrid)	*Rhododendron*
	Syngonium	*Syngonium*
	Violetta	*Viola*
Jess	Fuchsia	*Fuchsia*
Jezebel	Border auricula	*Primula auricula*
	Daffodil	*Narcissus*
	Fuchsia	*Fuchsia*
JoJo	Day lily	*Hemerocallis*
Joan	Chrysanthemum	*Dendranthema*
Joanna	Cape primrose	*Streptocarpus*
	Viola	*Viola*
Joanne	Alpine auricula	*Primula auricula*
	Perpetual carnation	*Dianthus*
	Rose (hybrid tea)	*Rosa*

Jocelyn	Rose (floribunda)	*Rosa*
Jodie	Viola	*Viola*
Johanna	Azalea	*Rhododendron*
	Farinose primula	*Primula*
	Tulip	*Tulipa*
Joy	Alpine auricula	*Primula auricula*
	Aubrieta	*Aubrieta*
	Cranesbill	*Geranium*
	Daffodil	*Narcissus*
	Geranium	*Pelargonium*
	Lily	*Lilium*
	Penstemon	*Penstemon*
	Pink	*Dianthus*
	Saxifrage	*Saxifraga*
Joyce	Auricula	*Primula auricula*
	Iris (Reticulata)	*Iris*

Judith	Cinquefoil	*Potentilla fruticosa*
	Michaelmas daisy	*Aster novi-belgii*
Judy	Magnolia	*Magnolia*
Julia	Chrysanthemum	*Dendranthema*
	Fuchsia	*Fuchsia*
	Geranium	*Pelargonium*
	Heather	*Calluna vulgaris*
	Michaelmas daisy	*Aster novi-belgii*
	Viola	*Viola*
Juliane	Oriental poppy	*Papaver orientale*
Julie	Cape primrose	*Streptocarpus*
	Geranium	*Pelargonium*
	Larch	*Larix x marschlinsii*
Juliet	Iris	*Iris*
	Michaelmas daisy	*Aster novi-belgii*
	Rose (perpetual)	*Rosa*
	Saxifrage	*Saxifraga*
Juliette	Croton	*Codiaeum variegatum*
June	Penstemon	*Penstemon*

Karen	Geranium	*Pelargonium*
	Michaelmas daisy	*Aster novi-belgii*
	Viola	*Viola*
Karin	Rhododendron (hybrid)	*Rhododendron*
Karine	Oriental poppy	*Papaver orientale*
Kate	Cranesbill	*Geranium*
	Viola	*Viola*
Katherine	Dumb cane	*Dieffenbachia seguine*
Kathleen	Rose (hybrid musk)	*Rosa*
Kathryn	Geranium	*Pelargonium*
	Myrtle	*Lophomyrtus x ralphii*
Kathy	Alpine auricula	*Primula auricula*
	Bellflower	*Campanula carpatica*
	Violetta	*Viola*
Katie	Camellia	*Camellia japonica*
	Rose (climbing)	*Rosa*

Katrina	Fuchsia	*Fuchsia*
Katja	Apple	*Malus domestica*
Katy	Apple	*Malus domestica*
Kelly Jo	Houseleek	*Sempervivum*
Kerrie	Viola	*Viola*
Kerry Anne	Fuchsia	*Fuchsia*
Kim	Alpine auricula	*Primula auricula*
	Cape primrose	*Streptocarpus*
	Rose (patio)	*Rosa*
Kimberley	Camellia	*Camellia japonica*
Kimberly	Fuchsia	*Fuchsia*
	Rhododendron (hybrid)	*Rhododendron*
Kirsty	Viola	*Viola*
Kitty	Camellia	*Camellia japonica*
Kizzy	Viola	*Viola*
Kristina	Michaelmas daisy	*Aster novi-belgii*

Larissa	Viola	*Viola*
Laura	Fuchsia	*Fuchsia*
	Geranium	*Pelargonium*
	Lily	*Lilium*
	Pink	*Dianthus*
	Rose (hybrid tea)	*Rosa*
	Viola	*Viola x cornuta*
Laura Jane	Rose (hybrid tea)	*Rosa*
Laurie	Fuchsia	*Fuchsia*
Lavender	Bellflower	*Campanula carpatica*
Laverna	Viola	*Viola*
Lavinia	Phlox	*Phlox subulata*
	Rose (climbing)	*Rosa*
	Viola	*Viola*
Lena	Broom	*Cytisus*

Lena	Fuchsia	*Fuchsia*
	Iris	*Iris*
Lenore	Geranium	*Pelargonium*
Leny	Rhododendron (hybrid)	*Rhododendron*
Leonora	Fuchsia	*Fuchsia*
	Spiderwort	*Tradescantia x andersoniana*
Leonore	Gladioli	*Gladiolus*
	Rhododendron (hybrid)	*Rhododendron*
	Saxifrage	*Saxifraga x landaueri*
Letitia	Geranium	*Pelargonium*
	Iris	*Iris sibirica*
	Mullein	*Verbascum*
	Viola	*Viola*
Lianne	Sweet violet	*Viola odorata*
Lilian	Geranium	*Pelargonium*
Liliana	Viola	*Viola*
Liliane	Houseleek	*Sempervivum*
Linda	Day lily	*Hemerocallis*
	Geranium	*Pelargonium*
	Rhododendron (hybrid)	*Rhododendron*

Lindsey	Geranium	*Pelargonium*
Lindy	Chrysanthemum	*Dendranthema*
Lisa	Alpine auricula	*Primula auricula*
	Cape primrose	*Streptocarpus*
	Fig	*Ficus carica*
	Fuchsia	*Fuchsia*
	Geranium	*Pelargonium*
Lisa Dawn	Michaelmas daisy	*Aster novi-belgii*
Lisbeth	Phlox	*Phlox x arendsii*
Livia	Violetta	*Viola*
Liz	Fuchsia	*Fuchsia*
	Ivy	*Hedera helix*
Lola	Viola	*Viola*
Lolita	Fuchsia	*Fuchsia*

Lorelei	Geranium	*Pelargonium*
Loretta	Geranium	*Pelargonium*
Lorna	Azalea	*Rhododendron*
	Delphinium	*Delphinium*
	Geranium	*Pelargonium*
	Viola	*Viola*
Lorraine	Chrysanthemum	*Dendranthema*
	Geranium	*Pelargonium*
Lotte	Azalea	*Rhododendron*
Louisa	Azalea	*Rhododendron*
	Plantain lily	*Hosta sieboldii*
	Viola	*Viola*
Louise	Chrysanthemum	*Dendranthema*
	Geranium	*Pelargonium*
Luca	Viola	*Viola*
Lucia	Crowberry	*Empetrum nigrum*
Lucilla	Geranium	*Pelargonium*
Lucille	Fuchsia	*Fuchsia*
Lucinda	Geranium	*Pelargonium*
	Viola	*Viola*
Lucy	Aubrieta	*Aubrieta*

Lucy *cont.*	Geranium	*Pelargonium*
	Michaelmas daisy	*Aster novi-belgii*
	Viola	*Viola*
Lulu	French marigold*	*Tagetes patula*
	Geranium	*Pelargonium*
	Lupin	*Lupinus*
	Viola	*Viola*
Lydia	Viola	*Viola*
Lyn	Tasmanian currant	*Coprosma petriei*
Lynette	Fuchsia	*Fuchsia*
	Lilac	*Syringa x josiflexa*
	Penstemon	*Penstemon*
Lynne	Cape primrose	*Streptocarpus*

Mabel	Ixia	*Ixia*
Madelaine	Daffodil	*Narcissus*
	Viola	*Viola*
Madeleine	Chrysanthemum	*Dendranthema*
Madge	Viola	*Viola*
Maggie	Viola	*Viola*
Mamie	Geranium	*Pelargonium*
Mandy	Pink	*Dianthus*
Manuela	Rose (hybrid tea)	*Rosa*
Marcia	Rhododendron (hybrid)	*Rhododendron*
Marella	Houseleek	*Sempervivum*
Margaret	Chrysanthemum	*Dendranthema*
	Fuchsia	*Fuchsia*
	Rose (hybrid tea)	*Rosa*
	Viola	*Viola*
Margarete	Windflower	*Anemone x hybrida*

Margarita	Fuchsia	*Fuchsia*
Margot	Sneezeweed	*Helenium*
Margret	Hebe	*Hebe*
Maria	Chrysanthemum	*Dendranthema*
	Clematis	*Clematis alpina*
	Pink	*Dianthus*
Marian	Viola	*Viola*
Marianna	Saxifrage	*Saxifraga x borisii*
Marie	Azalea	*Rhododendron*
	Chinese evergreen	*Aglaonema crispum*
	Hot-water plant	*Achimenes*
	Hyacinth	*Hyacinthus orientalis*
Marieke	Japanese spindle	*Euonymus japonicus*
Mariette	Tulip (lily)	*Tulipa*
Marigold	Primula (double)	*Primula auricula*
Marika	Viola	*Viola*
Marilee	Azalea	*Rhododendron*
Mariloo	Rhododendron (hybrid)	*Rhododendron*
Marilyn	Plantain lily	*Hosta*
Marion	Chrysanthemum	*Dendranthema*
	Geranium	*Pelargonium*
	Rhododendron (hybrid)	*Rhododendron*
Marinka	Camellia	*Camellia japonica*
	Fuchsia	*Fuchsia*

Marjorie	Clematis	*Clematis montana*
	Hebe	*Hebe*
	Michaelmas daisy	*Aster novi-belgii*
	Phlox	*Phlox subulata*
Marleen	Heather	*Calluna vulgaris*
Marlena	Rose (patio)	*Rosa*
Martha	Rose (bourbon)	*Rosa*
	Saxifrage	*Saxifraga x semmleri*
Martina	Yarrow	*Achillea*
Martine	Azalea	*Rhododendron*
Marty	Fuchsia	*Fuchsia*
Mary	Chrysanthemum	*Dendranthema*
	Fuchsia	*Fuchsia*

Mary *cont.*	Michaelmas daisy	*Aster novi-belgii*
	Primula (double)	*Primula auricula*
	Rose (polyantha)	*Rosa*
Mary Belle	Rhododendron (hybrid)	*Rhododendron*
Mary Ellen	Viola	*Viola*
Mary Helen	Azalea	*Rhododendron*
Mary Jo	Plantain lily	*Hosta*
Mary Lou	Daffodil	*Narcissus*
Mary Rose	Rose (shrub)	*Rosa*
Maureen	Clematis	*Clematis*
	Geranium	*Pelargonium*
	Tulip	*Tulipa*
Mavis	Chrysanthemum	*Dendranthema*
Mayleen	Clematis	*Clematis montana*
Meena	Violetta	*Viola*
Meg	Rose (climbing)	*Rosa*
Megan	Azalea	*Rhododendron*

Melanie	Geranium	*Pelargonium*
	Houseleek	*Sempervivum*
	Ivy	*Hedera helix*
Melina	Rose (hybrid tea)	*Rosa*
Melinda	Violetta	*Viola*
Melissa	Begonia	*Begonia*
	Bergamot	*Monarda*
	Forsythia	*Forsythia*
	Geranium	*Pelargonium*
	Viola	*Viola*
Melody	Fuchsia	*Fuchsia*
Melody Ann	Fuchsia	*Fuchsia*
Merrill	Magnolia	*Magnolia x loebneri*
Mia	Geranium	*Pelargonium*
Michelle	Geranium	*Pelargonium*
	Michaelmas daisy	*Aster novi-belgii*
Millie	Geranium	*Pelargonium*

Mimi	Azalea	*Rhododendron*
	Geranium	*Pelargonium*
	Rose (miniature)	*Rosa*
Miranda	Fairy's thimble	*Campanula cochleariifolia*
	Geranium	*Pelargonium*
	Hydrangea	*Hydrangea serrata*
	Michaelmas daisy	*Aster novi-belgii*
	Violetta	*Viola*
Mireille	Grape vine	*Vitis vinifera*
Mirella	Gladioli	*Gladiolus*
Mitzi	Geranium	*Pelargonium*
Modesty	Geranium	*Pelargonium*
Moira	Chrysanthemum	*Dendranthema*
Mollie	Geranium	*Pelargonium*
Molly Ann	Rhododendron (hybrid)	*Rhododendron*
Mona	Aeschynanthus	*Aeschynanthus*
Monica	Hebe	*Hebe*
	Rhododendron (hybrid)	*Rhododendron*
	Viola	*Viola*

Morgan	Maple	*Acer rubrum*
Morwenna	Geranium	*Pelargonium*
	Viola	*Viola*
Moyra	Fuchsia	*Fuchsia*
Muriel	Fuchsia	*Fuchsia*
	Geranium	*Pelargonium*
	Rhododendron (hybrid)	*Rhododendron*
Myfawnny	Viola	*Viola*
Myra	Rose (hybrid tea)	*Rosa*
	Saxifrage	*Saxifraga x anglica*
Myriam	Rose (hybrid tea)	*Rosa*

Nadine	Geranium	*Pelargonium*
Nana	Wormwood	*Artemesia stelleriana*
Nancy	Michaelmas daisy	*Aster novi-belgii*
Nancy Lou	Fuchsia	*Fuchsia*
Nanette	Geranium	*Pelargonium*
Nannette	Houseleek	*Jovibarba heuffelii*
Naomi	Chrysanthemum	*Dendranthema*
	Eucodonia	*Eucodonia andrieuxii*
	Geranium	*Pelargonium*
	Rhododendron (hybrid)	*Rhododendron*
Natasha	Erodium	*Erodium x kolbianum*
Nathalie	Chrysanthemum	*Dendranthema*
Nella	Geranium	*Pelargonium*
Nellie	Geranium	*Pelargonium*
Nerissa	Snowdrop	*Galanthus*
Nettie	Azalea	*Rhododendron*

Nicola	Cape primrose	*Streptocarpus*
	Fuchsia	*Fuchsia*
	Plantain lily (Tardiana)	*Hosta*
	Rose (floribunda)	*Rosa*
Nicole	Chrysanthemum	*Dendranthema*
	Gladioli	*Gladiolus*
Niki	Broom	*Cytisus x kewensis*
Nikki	Fuchsia	*Fuchsia*
Nina	Perpetual carnation	*Dianthus*
Norah	Alpine auricula	*Primula auricula*
Noreen	Dahlia (pompon)	*Dahlia*
Norma	Alpine auricula	*Primula auricula*
	Azalea	*Rhododendron*

Olga	Geranium	*Pelargonium*
	Rhododendron (hybrid)	*Rhododendron*
Olive	Rhododendron (hybrid)	*Rhododendron*
Olivia	Lily	*Lilium*
Opal	Anchusa	*Anchusa azurea*
Ophelia	Azalea	*Rhododendron*
	Rose (hybrid tea)	*Rosa*

Pamela	Chrysanthemum	*Dendranthema*
	Italian bellflower	*Campanula isophylla*
	Michaelmas daisy	*Aster novi-belgii*
	Water lily	*Nymphaea*
Pandora	Lily	*Lilium*
	Rhododendron (hybrid)	*Rhododendron*
	Rose	*Rosa*
	Strawberry	*Fragaria x ananassa*
Pat	Auricula (show)	*Primula auricula*
	Chrysanthemum	*Dendranthema*
	Rock rose	*Cistus ladanifer*
Patience	Auricula (show)	*Primula auricula*
	Fuchsia	*Fuchsia*
Patricia	Apple (dessert)	*Malus domestica*
	Border carnation	*Dianthus*
	Chrysanthemum	*Dendranthema*

Patricia *cont.*	Fuchsia	*Fuchsia*
	Hot-water plant	*Achimenes*
	Rose (floribunda)	*Rosa*
Paula	Cape primrose	*Streptocarpus*
	Lewisia	*Lewisia*
	Saxifrage	*Saxifraga x paulinae*
Paulina	Forsythia	*Forsythia*
Pauline	Clematis	*Clematis macropetala*
	Geranium	*Pelargonium*
	Iris (Reticulata)	*Iris*
	Spiderwort	*Tradescantia x andersoniana*
Peggy	Alpine auricula	*Primula auricula*
	Chrysanthemum	*Dendranthema*

Peggy Sue	Geranium	*Pelargonium*
Penelope	Rhododendron (hybrid)	*Rhododendron hybrid*
	Rose (hybrid musk)	*Rosa*
	Saxifrage	*Saxifraga x boydilacina*
Penny	Geranium	*Pelargonium*
	Marguerite	*Argyranthemum*
Perdita	Rose (shrub)	*Rosa*
Petra	Heather	*Calluna vulgaris*
	Saxifrage	*Saxifraga*
Phoebe	Azalea	*Rhododendron*
	Rose (shrub)	*Rosa*
Phyllis	Fuchsia	*Fuchsia*
	Gentian	*Gentiana asclepiadea*
	Penstemon	*Penstemon*
Pia	Hydrangea	*Hydrangea macrophylla*
Polly	Erodium	*Erodium sebaceum*
	Rose (hybrid tea)	*Rosa*

Primrose	Begonia	*Begonia*
Priscilla	Gladioli	*Gladiolus*
Prudence	Geranium	*Pelargonium*
	Pink	*Dianthus*
Prunella	Michaelmas daisy	*Aster novi-belgii*
Purity	Cosmos	*Cosmos*

| Queeny | Dahlia | *Dahlia* |

Rachael	Hot-water plant	*Achimenes*
Rachel	Geranium	*Pelargonium*
	Heather	*Erica x watsonii*
	Pink	*Dianthus*
Ramona	Clematis	*Clematis*
	Rose (climbing)	*Rosa*
Raquel	Chrysanthemum	*Dendranthema*
Rebecca	Escallonia	*Escallonia*
	Geranium	*Pelargonium*
	Violetta	*Viola*
Rhoda	Viola	*Viola*
Rhonda	Dahlia (pompon)	*Dahlia*
Ricki	Magnolia	*Magnolia*
Rita Jane	Houseleek	*Sempervivum*
Robin	Geranium	*Pelargonium*
Romy	Rhododendron (hybrid)	*Rhododendron*

Rona	Irish ivy	*Hedera hibernica*
Rosabell	Rose (patio)	*Rosa*
Rosabella	Arabis	*Arabis caucasica*
	Spanish bluebell	*Hyacinthoides hispanica*
Rosaleen	Geranium	*Pelargonium*
Rosalie	Geranium	*Pelargonium*
	Hyacinth	*Hyacinthus orientalis*
	Maple	*Acer davidii*
Rosalind	Gaultheria	*Gaultheria mucronata*
	Heather	*Calluna vulgaris*
Rosalinda	Azalea	*Rhododendron*
Rosalinde	Phlox	*Phlox maculata*
	Veronica	*Veronica*

Rosamund	Auricula (double)	*Primula auricula*
	Lobelia*	*Lobelia*
Rosamunda	Geranium	*Pelargonium*
	Saxifrage	*Saxifraga*
Rosanna	Auricula (show)	*Primula auricula*
Rosanne	Plantain lily	*Hosta*
Rose	Anthurium	*Anthurium andreanum*
	Cranesbill	*Geranium endressii*
	Forget me not*	*Myosotis*
	Purple loosestrife	*Lythrum salicaria*
Rose Marie	Fuchsia	*Fuchsia*
Rosealie	Pink	*Dianthus*
Rosemarie	Anthurium	*Anthurium scherzerianum*
	Saxifrage	*Saxifraga x anglica*
Rosemary	Auricula (show)	*Primula auricula*
Rosie	Gaultheria	*Gaultheria mucronata*
	Houseleek	*Sempervivum*
Rosina	Rose (miniature)	*Rosa*

Rosita	Chrysanthemum	*Dendranthema*
	Geranium	*Pelargonium*
	Hydrangea	*Hydrangea macrophylla*
	Lily	*Lilium*
Rowena	Alpine auricula	*Primula auricula*
Ruby	Cape primrose	*Streptocarpus*
	Clematis	*Clematis alpina*
	Delphinium	*Delphinium*
	Fuchsia	*Fuchsia*
	Geranium	*Pelargonium*
	Heather	*Erica cinerea*
	Hot-water plant	*Achimenes*
	Magnolia	*Magnolia*
	Penstemon	*Penstemon*
	Pink	*Dianthus*
Rusty	Geranium	*Pelargonium*
	Houseleek	*Sempervivum*
Ruth	Cinquefoil	*Potentilla fruticosa*
	Houseleek	*Sempervivum*
	Pink	*Dianthus*
	Rhodohypoxis	*Rhodohypoxis*

Sable	Iris	*Iris*
Sabrina	Camellia	*Camellia japonica*
	Cotoneaster	*Cotoneaster splendens*
	Delphinium	*Delphinium*
Sally	Ivy	*Hedera helix*
Sally Ann	Fuchsia	*Fuchsia*
Sally Anne	Geranium	*Pelargonium*
Salome	Alpine auricula	*Primula auricula*
	Daffodil	*Narcissus*
Sam	Iris	*Iris*
Samantha	Camellia	*Camellia reticulata*
	Daffodil	*Narcissus*
	Delphinium	*Delphinium*
	Geranium	*Pelargonium*
Sandra	Alpine auricula	*Primula auricula*

Sandra	Cape primrose	*Streptocarpus*
	Witch Hazel	*Hamamelis vernalis*
Sandy	Chrysanthemum	*Dendranthema*
Sara Helen	Fuchsia	*Fuchsia*
Sarah	Calico bush	*Kalmia latifolia*
	Cape primrose	*Streptocarpus*
	Chrysanthemum	*Dendranthema*
	Daffodil	*Narcissus*
	Rose (hybrid tea)	*Rosa*
Sasha	Geranium	*Pelargonium*
Saskia	Chrysanthemum	*Dendranthema*
	Fuchsia	*Fuchsia*
Selina	Geranium	*Pelargonium*
Sharon	Geranium	*Pelargonium*
Sheena	Michaelmas daisy	*Aster novi-belgii*
Sheila	Auricula (show)	*Primula auricula*
	Chrysanthemum	*Dendranthema*
	Geranium	*Pelargonium*
Shelley	Geranium	*Pelargonium*

Sherry	Heather	*Erica carnea*
Shirley	Chrysanthemum	*Dendranthema*
	Heather	*Calluna vulgaris*
	Tulip	*Tulipa*
Shona	Rose (floribunda)	*Rosa*
Simona	Rhododendron (hybrid)	*Rhododendron*
Siobhan	Fuchsia	*Fuchsia*
Sonia	Dahlia	*Dahlia*
	Michaelmas daisy	*Aster amellus*

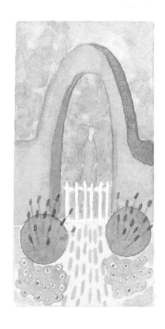

Sonya	Alpine auricula	*Primula auricula*
Sophia	Michaelmas daisy	*Aster novi-belgii*
Stella	Auricula (show)	*Primula auricula*
	Bellflower	*Campanula poscharskyana*
	Cape primrose	*Streptocarpus*
	Honesty	*Lunaria annua*
	Rhododendron (hybrid)	*Rhododendron*
	Rhodohypoxis	*Rhodohypoxis*
	Rose (hybrid tea)	*Rosa*
	Saxifrage	*Saxifraga x stormonthii*
	Wild cherry	*Prunus avium*
Stephanie	Erodium	*Erodium*
	Rhododendron (hybrid)	*Rhododendron*
Sue	Alpine auricula	*Primula auricula*
	Hot-water plant	*Achimenes*
Susan	Alpine auricula	*Primula auricula*
	Cape primrose	*Streptocarpus*
	Fuchsia	*Fuchsia*
	Gentian	*Gentiana*
	Geranium	*Pelargonium*
	Magnolia	*Magnolia*
	Pink	*Dianthus*
	Rhododendron (hybrid)	*Rhododendron*

Susannah	Auricula (double)	*Primula auricula*
	Pink	*Dianthus*
Susie	Black-eyed Susan*	*Thunbergia alata*
Suzanne	Ivy	*Hedera helix*
Suzie	Bellflower	*Campanula carpatica*
Suzy	Daffodil	*Narcissus*
	Fuchsia	*Fuchsia*
Sybilla	Hydrangea	*Hydrangea macrophylla*
Sybille	Mock orange	*Philadelphus*
Sylvia	Camellia	*Camellia japonica*
	Geranium	*Pelargonium*
Sylvy	Fuchsia	*Fuchsia*

Tabatha	Fuchsia	*Fuchsia*
Tamara	Lily	*Lilium*
Tammy	Geranium	*Pelargonium*
Tania	Lobelia	*Lobelia*
Tanya	Camellia	*Camellia sasanqua*
	Fuchsia	*Fuchsia*
	Geranium	*Pelargonium*
Tara	Ginger lily	*Hedychium coccineum*
	Rhododendron (hybrid)	*Rhododendron*
Teresa	Hot-water plant	*Achimenes*
Tess	Irish ivy	*Hedera hibernica*
Tessa	Flaming Katy	*Kalanchoe blossfeldiana*
	Rhododendron (hybrid)	*Rhododendron*
Thalia	Daffodil	*Narcissus*
	Fuchsia	*Fuchsia*
Thalia	Rose	*Rosa*

Thea	Geranium	*Pelargonium*
Thelma	Rose (rambler)	*Rosa*
Thisbe	Rose (hybrid musk)	*Rosa*
Thora	Pink	*Dianthus*
Tiffany	Camellia	*Camellia japonica*
	Fuchsia	*Fuchsia*
	Geranium	*Pelargonium*
	Houseleek	*Sempervivum*
Tilly	Geranium	*Pelargonium*
Tina	Cape primrose	*Streptocarpus*
	Heather	*Erica tetralix*
	Houseleek	*Sempervivum*
Toni	Geranium	*Pelargonium*
Tonia	Hinoki cypress	*Chamaecyparis obtusa*
Topaz	Fuchsia	*Fuchsia*
	Houseleek	*Sempervivum*
Tracey	Cape primrose	*Streptocarpus*

Traci Sue	Houseleek	*Sempervivum*
Tracie Ann	Fuchsia	*Fuchsia*
Tracy	Geranium	*Pelargonium*
Trixie	Hebe	*Hebe*
Trudie	Geranium	*Pelargonium*
Trudy	Auricula (show)	*Primula auricula*
	Fuchsia	*Fuchsia*

| Unity | Fleabane | *Erigeron* |
| Ursula | French marigold* | *Tagetes patula* |

Valentina	Geranium	*Pelargonium*
Valerie	Alpine auricula	*Primula auricula*
	Geranium	*Pelargonium*
Vanessa	Fuchsia	*Fuchsia*
	Hot-water plant	*Achimenes*
	Rhododendron (hybrid)	*Rhododendron*
Venetia	Azalea	*Rhododendron*
	Saxifrage	*Saxifraga paniculata*
Venus	False goat's beard	*Astilbe x arendsii*
	Geranium	*Pelargonium*
Vera	Amaryllis	*Hippeastrum*
	Clematis	*Clematis montana*
	Hydrangea	*Hydrangea paniculata*
	Iris	*Iris*
	Marguerite	*Argyranthemum*
Veronica	Geranium	*Pelargonium*

Victoria	Clematis	*Clematis*
	Gooseberry	*Ribes uva-crispa*
	Heather	*Erica cinerea*
	Magnolia	*Magnolia grandiflora*
	Plum	*Prunus domestica*
	Rhubarb	*Rheum x hybridum*
	Salvia	*Salvia farinacea*
Violet	Bellflower	*Campanula lactiflora*
	Houseleek	*Jovibarba heuffelii*
Violetta	Abutilon	*Abutilon x suntense*
	Azalea	*Rhododendron*
	Hot-water plant	*Achimenes*
	Knapweed	*Centauria montana*
	Michaelmas daisy	*Aster novae-angliae*
	Sea lavender	*Limonium platyphyllum*
Violette	Rose (rambler)	*Rosa*
Virginia	Chrysanthemum	*Dendranthema*
	Geranium	*Pelargonium*
Vita	Viola	*Viola*
Vivien	Iris	*Iris*

Wanda	Aubrieta	*Aubrieta*
	Heather	*Erica carnea*
	Primrose	*Primula*
	Viola	*Viola*
Wendy	Chrysanthemum	*Dendranthema*
	Fuchsia	*Fuchsia*
	Geranium	*Pelargonium*
	Houseleek	*Sempervivum*
	Kalanchoe	*Kalanchoe*
	Saxifrage	*Saxifraga x wendelacina*
	Speedwell	*Veronica spicata incana*
Wilma	Hot-water plant	*Achimenes*
Winifred	Cape primrose	*Streptocarpus*

Winifred *cont.*	Phlox	*Phlox subulata*
	Saxifrage	*Saxifraga x anglica*
Winifrid	Alpine auricula	*Primula auricula*
Winona	Violetta	*Viola*

Yolanda	Geranium	*Pelargonium*
Yvonne	Bellflower	*Campanula*
	Dahlia	*Dahlia*
	Geranium	*Pelargonium*
	Heather	*Erica cinerea*
	Lawson cypress	*Chamaecyparis lawsoniana*
	Rhododendron (hybrid)	*Rhododendron*

Zara	Day lily	*Hemerocallis*
	Fuchsia	*Fuchsia*
	Viola	*Viola*
Zeta	Viola	*Viola*
Zoe	Geranium	*Pelargonium*
	Violetta	*Viola*
Zola	Rose (shrub)	*Rosa*
Zowie	Iris	*Iris*